Praise fo

"I've known and worked with Larry H_____
Larry has a great depth of kindness_____
Larry proposes an idea—whether_____
kids—you know that he and his w_____
and create an amazing experience for kids. Then, Larry is going to ____
side and let everyone else take the credit!"

—ROB CONNOLLY, President, Boys & Girls Clubs of San Francisco

"Larry has been an incredible mentor to me as I have built the MeWater Foundation. His passion towards unconditional giving is beyond inspiring as well as his
willingness to share his insights and experiences with me. When I grow up, I want
to be Larry Harper. Thanks for everything!"

–EDDIE DONNELLAN, Founder MeWater Foundation

"It was an absolute pleasure working with Larry Harper to design a space for our
young artists to create music and memories. His professionalism, knowledge, and
integrity made the process smooth and fun—even in a pandemic! I admire all he
does for nonprofits in helping them with their mission and vision."

—MELISSA GROVE, Director of Programming & Officer of Joyous Possibilities,
Jason Mraz Foundation

"Larry is a leader in the nonprofit world. He is accomplished, well-connected, and,
most importantly, passionate. Anyone who is interested in learning more about the
non-profit world, and specifically how to run a successful and impactful charity,
should take advantage of the chance to learn from Larry!"

—HEATHER HOOPER, Director of Community Relations and the
San Jose Sharks Foundation.

"The Muhammad Ali Center worked with Larry and his Good Tidings Foundation
on a project to renovate an art studio and provide art supplies to Central High
School; the high school Muhammad Ali attended as a teenager. Larry approached
the project with great joy and a pure heart. His only goal was to make the world
a better place for the students at Central High School, proving that he is truly a
great humanitarian."

—DONALD LASSERE, President & CEO, Muhammad Ali Center

"You learn best from someone who loves what they do—and Larry has always put
his heart and soul into what he does. Having built the Good Tidings Foundation
from a simple act of goodwill, Larry knew that one person (or two, along with wife,
Ronnie) could truly make a difference in the lives of others. With that philosophy
giving him firm footing as a grassroots philanthropist, Larry truly has a genuine
voice when both fundraising and building partnerships. As someone who wants
to keep giving, Larry is a natural teacher for others in the nonprofit world. I
know you'll be inspired by his approach to community work and his advice for
maintaining a vibrant organization."

—SUE PETERSEN, Executive Director, San Francisco Giants Community Fund

"Larry Harper is a true humanitarian at his core. His clever approach to fundraising and nonprofit management are a breath of fresh air to donors looking to make a big impact. Within a few minutes of meeting him, he'll gain your trust and make you want to ask how you can help. This book shares what it really takes to start and establish a prominent charity in these ever-changing times."
—STACY McCORKLE, Director of Community Relations, San Francisco 49ers.

"Larry Harper is a person who is quiet and mild-mannered, but powerful. When he speaks, his words will always contain wisdom, insight, and truth. Alice Cooper's Solid Rock organization has been the recipient of Larry's counsel and generosity for over twenty years. We have benefited from his vast knowledge of non-profits' inner workings, the brilliance of his fundraising acumen, and his love for people, especially kids. Mr. Harper is the go-to source for creating and sustaining a successful nonprofit organization, sticking to mission and vision while thinking outside the box. He helps to make you and your organization better, stronger, and more focused."
—JEFF MOORE, Executive Director/VP, Alice Cooper's Solid Rock Teen Centers, Inc

"Faith, passion, dedication, sacrifice, commitment, and celebration are just a few words that describe the doctrine of sports fandom, and Larry Harper. Larry brings his life's calling in and utter love for sports, coupled with his philanthropic spirit, to the conversation every single time. Larry channeled his devotion, passion, and commitments to improving the lives of vulnerable youth twenty-seven years ago when he started his nonprofit Good Tidings Foundation, a foundation that furnishes access for youth in marginalized communities to thrive through sports, the arts, and education. His tremendous success in the nonprofit environment makes Larry the perfect individual to write the handbook on how to start and grow a charity. I, for one, will refer to his text like my team's playbook during the Super Bowl."
—KRIS PRIMACIO, CEO, International Surf Therapy Organization

"CC and I have had the pleasure to partner with multiple nonprofits through The PitCCh In Foundation. One of our longest standing relationships has been with Good Tidings and its founder, Larry Harper. We all believe change begins with the youth and that's why our missions both align with providing them with a safe place to strive for success through education and athletic activities. Having Larry's support on both the West and East Coasts has proven his commitment to the youth. Thank you for continuing to serve, support and advocate for our future, The Youth!
—AMBER SABATHIA, Cofounder, PitCCh In Foundation

"Larry Harper has an uncanny ability to identify and connect with individuals nationwide. Through the Good Tidings Foundation, he nurtures partnership to other organizations in providing scholarships and facilities for underserved communities. His tips and tricks in this book will help you elevate your cause."
—TARA ZABOR, Executive Director, LeRoy Neiman and Janet Byrne Neiman Foundation

So You Want to Start a
CHARITY

So You Want to Start a
CHARITY

Your One-Hour
Can't-Miss Guide

LARRY HARPER

Cover and interior design by Tabitha Lahr
Interior illustrations © Shutterstock.com

Published 2021
Published by the Good Tidings Foundation
www.goodtidings.org

Printed in the United States of America

Print ISBN: 978-0-692-90792-4
Library of Congress Control Number: 2020910741

Want to chat more about your charity? Contact Larry at
larry@goodtidings.org

Listen to all sorts of amazing people
doing good on the Good Tidings Podcast:
https://goodtidings.org/podcastandnews.

GOOD TIDINGS
PODCAST

100% of sales from this book to be
donated to the Good Tidings Foundation

For all the
dreamers
and do-gooders
in the world!

Contents

Preface

In a perfect world, charities would not be needed. There would be no poverty, disease would be unheard-of, the climate would be forever perfect, all countries would help one another whenever they were in need, and wars would be the stuff of fantasy.

But as we all know, we don't live in a perfect world. Poverty not only exists, it affects a staggering number of people around the globe; an estimated 10 percent of the world's population lives in extreme poverty, and hundreds of millions more struggle to feed their families and keep a roof over their heads each day. Disease has been front and center for the last year and a half as the COVID-19 pandemic has ravaged countries big and small. Climate change is changing the face of our planet, causing extreme weather events and, in some places, driving people from their homes. Countries tend not to offer help to one another unless there's something in it for them. And wars . . . well, we know the answer to that one.

So, charities? Yeah, we need them.

This book is *not* designed as a technical how-to. It doesn't lay out how to become a 501(c)3 in a micro, step-by-step way. What it does cover are tried-and-tested ways to think outside of the box and create a well-supported mission that will last for generations. The words on the pages that follow will hopefully inspire you to start, nurture, and grow a charity you will be proud of, and encourage you to do so in your own unique way.

I have had the desire to write this book for some time. I am finally composing it now in a tumultuous time: in my home, under a shelter-in-place order, in the middle of the coronavirus pandemic, at the same time that racial justice rallies seeking to spark positive change for America's Black community are blooming all over the US. This is an intense, fraught time in our country. But the good news that I know will come out of all this is that when we emerge from this moment of crisis, just like in the aftermath of 9/11, there will be a fervor of charitable giving. New movements will form as a new generation of people are inspired into a life of service and begin to create new, and much-needed, charities.

We live in an imperfect world, but we're all in this together. So as long as we are all inhabiting this imperfect place, I feel it is our responsibility to do what we can to lend a helping hand to both our planet and to one another. We are *all* born with kind and loving hearts—so let's use them for good!

Chapter 1:

So I Started a Charity

It was the summer of 1994 and life was grand. A gallon of gas cost around a buck. The average price of a house in the US was $100,000. It was an excellent year for movies; *Forrest Gump*, *The Lion King*, and *Speed* had all recently premiered. And Major League Baseball was headed for an epic finish to a special season—which, since I was the Scouting Supervisor for the Seattle Mariners at the time, was of particular interest to me.

It was Thursday, August 11th, and I was driving down Highway 101 to attend a San Jose Giants Minor League Baseball game. I was listening to the DJs on the local sports talk radio station bantering back and forth about who was the best player in the Major Leagues as I drove—and then, suddenly, a newsflash interrupted their chatter: *"The remainder of the Major League Baseball season and World Series has been cancelled!"*

It was the most embarrassing day in the history of baseball. The owners of Major League Baseball teams were proposing a salary cap for players; the players were refusing to accept the cap. Essentially, rich team owners and rich baseball players couldn't agree on how rich they wanted to be. It killed the Montreal Expos franchise, ended Michael Jordan's baseball career, and destroyed Tony Gwynn's chance to catch up to the great Ted Williams as the next .400 hitter.

I didn't know all this was to come when I first heard the news on the radio, of course—but my stomach still sank. Never in my lifetime had something like this happened, and the first thing that popped into my head when I heard it was, *What must kids who love baseball be thinking?* All those young girls and boys who played softball or Little League and who loved watching the pros play—they must be so disappointed. *If this had happened when I was a kid, how would it have affected my dreams?* I wondered. *Is this going to tarnish these young people's opinion of this great game?*

I should write a children's book about baseball. The thought popped into my head out of nowhere, but once it was there, I couldn't get it out. I felt I had to do it.

This was, objectively, a ridiculous idea. I was *not* a writer. I'd never gotten better than a B-minus in high school English, and I certainly hadn't done anything to become a better writer since then. Words were not my thing. And now here I was, wanting to write a children's book. What was I thinking?

Yet still, I couldn't get the idea out of my head—and the longer it was in there, the more it kept growing and solidifying. I knew it should be for children ages five to twelve. I knew it should be a book parents could read to their kids at bedtime. When I remembered a past *Sports Illustrated* story that featured about a dozen Rockwell-esque baseball images by an artist named Brent Benger—illustrations of a boy playing catch with his dad in the front yard, a girl getting picked for a team before a boy, a kid listening to his favorite team on the radio while falling asleep with his head on a pillow—I knew those drawings would make the perfect imagery for a child to sink into and dream about. I knew I wanted to write short poems to go with each of those images. And I also knew that once the book became a reality, I wanted to give 100% of its sales to youth charities: the Jackie Robinson Foundation, the Make A Wish Foundation, and others like them.

I might be crazy, but I had a plan. So, once my vision came together, I wasted no time. I gathered the images and wrote the poems in short order, and soon . . . I had a book!

Only one problem. No one would buy a book from Larry Harper, because no one had any idea who Larry Harper was. I needed some star power if I was going to get this thing out into the world.

After giving some thought to exactly whose star power would be right for this book, I wrote a letter to Vin Scully—the very private man who'd spent sixty-seven years broadcasting Los Angeles Dodger games and telling amazing stories night after night, maybe the most iconic person in all of Los Angeles, and, it just so happened, my childhood idol. It felt like a long shot, but I knew he was exactly the person I needed. So I gave the letter to a friend of mine who was a coach for the Dodgers, and he gave it to Vin. After that, all I could do was wait.

Lucky for me, I didn't have to wait long. Just three days later, there was a message on my answering machine: "Hello Larry, this is Vin Scully. I love your book idea. I would love to write the foreword and I will even ask my friend Peter O'Malley, the owner of our ball club, if he can help get it printed and published."

My jaw dropped. Unbelievable—one of the most famous people in all of sports was now part of this project! I couldn't believe my good luck.

Long story short: Vin was true to his word, we got the book published, it sold well (to date, three editions have sold out), and we raised a considerable amount of money for a number of deserving charities.

I could have stopped there. I'd had an idea, I'd seen it through, and I'd achieved even more than I'd believed I could. But as I witnessed the book's success, it became clear to me that I wanted to keep going—wanted to do even more good, keep helping children

in some way. I started thinking about the best way to do that, and the following January, along with my wife Ronette, the Good Tidings Foundation was born.

In Good Tidings' first year, we delivered toys to children in deserving neighborhoods in the San Francisco Bay Area. In our second year, we enlisted the Golden State Warriors Basketball Team to throw a party for homeless children with us (we would supply the toys, they would provide the professional basketball players). Following that wonderful event, David Hatfield, their Director of Community Relations, asked if we would like to partner with them to refurbish an inner-city basketball court—which we knew nothing about. Now, twenty-seven years later, we have built nearly 100 courts with the Warriors and well over 200 athletic, art, and music spaces for marginalized children in Northern California and beyond.

The constant thought that has spurred my efforts on from the beginning of my philanthropic work is that children have no choice about the circumstances they're born into. No one *deserves* to be poor, just as no one *deserves* wealth or good fortune. If you have it, good for you. You may have worked very hard for what you have. But some people are born with the deck stacked against them, and for every good fortune in the world, there is also hardship. Moreover opportunity is not spread perfectly evenly throughout the world. So it's the job of those of us in more privileged positions to help make things more even and help others regardless of what their need might be where possible.

It is my belief that we are all born with kind and loving hearts—that it's human nature to want to help where help is needed.

Are YOU ready to help?

Chapter 2:

Passion vs. Obsession

During your lifetime, you will undoubtedly become passionate about a cause.

passion [**pash**-*uh*n] *noun.* any compelling emotion or feeling.

Nearly everyone has a passion for *something* that has a philanthropic element to it, whether it's to save an endangered species, provide a meal for a homeless person, help a town in Africa access clean water, lend a hand to a wounded veteran, gift a toy to a child during the holidays, or something else. Passion is the emotion that can move you to a volunteer or donor state—what gets you fired up about taking action to help effect change where change is needed.

Every charity needs passionate supporters. And there's not just one way to provide this support; there are many ways. Do you have a little time to spare and experience sitting on a committee of some sort? You can serve as a board member. Are you short on time but have a deep wallet? Consider acting as a fiscal sponsor. Are you a hands-on, nose-to-the-grindstone type? Helping stuff envelopes for an annual donor appeal is a great way to contribute.

If you'd like to start your own cause and have the means but not much spare time to give, think about starting a donor-advised fund. A donor-advised fund is like a charitable investment account with the sole purpose of supporting charitable organizations you care about. When you contribute cash, securities, or other assets to a donor-advised fund at a public charity like Vanguard Charitable, Schwab Charitable, or Fidelity Charitable, you are generally eligible to take an immediate tax deduction. Then those funds can be invested for tax-free growth and you can recommend grants to virtually any IRS-qualified public charity. Using this approach, you don't have to keep track of every gift acknowledgment from every charity you support—your donor-advised fund holder will provide all your required forms for your tax records. And yet another advantage of this type of fund is that you can incorporate it into your estate planning; if you want to ensure that your giving will go on in perpetuity, you can simply make a bequest in your will to the donor-advised fund sponsor.

This is a very simple way to create your own mini private charity, and you don't have to be rich to do it; you can get started with a contribution as small as $5,000. This is a great option for the passionate person.

Passion is one thing; obsession is another. And though the latter often gets a bad rap, in my experience truly successful charities are those started by founders who exceed the passion level to become head-over-heels obsessed with their cause. Passion can start you down the road toward philanthropic involvement, but it will only get you so far. In the end, only obsession is enough to make you stay the course no matter what obstacles come your way.

> **obsession** [*uh*b-**sesh**-*uh*n] *noun.* thoughts or feelings of a persistent idea, image or desire that dominates your thoughts.

There is no doubt that Dr. Martin Luther King Jr. was obsessed with his cause; fueled by his faith and deep convictions, he lived and breathed it and even, in the end, laid down his life for it. Candace Lightner, the founder of Mothers Against Drunk Driving was obsessed with her mission for obvious personal reasons: her own daughter was struck and killed by a drunk driver at just thirteen years old, after which Lightner made educating the public about the dangers of drunk driving her personal crusade. In this context, obsession, for me, has a positive connotation, even if (as in the case of Candace Lightner) the reason for the obsession is a sad one. Why? Because neither King nor Lightner would ever have reached the number of people they did if obsession with their cause hadn't driven them to do so.

What is the obsession that will move you to good? This is the inner fire you must draw upon when you're forming a nonprofit. And it needs to be a *real* fire, not a narrative you've invented or exaggerated because you know it will sound good to other people. Creating a successful charity can be as difficult as becoming a rock star or a renowned artist—and if your motivation isn't sincere, it won't work. For one thing, if you're not genuine, potential donors will pick up on that and won't feel moved to give. For another, working on getting things up and running will initially be so time-consuming that it will essentially be your lifestyle—so you'd better care, *really* care, about what you're doing, or you'll lose steam quickly.

If you're paying attention to health experts and sleeping the recommended eight hours a night, that leaves you sixteen hours a day to devote to the pursuit of your mission. Yes, I said *sixteen*. There are no forty-hour work weeks in this profession. Are you willing to use the time available to you to make your dreams a reality? 16 x 7 = 112. Those are the hours available in each and every week for you to make things happen!

Perseverance is the name of the game in the charity world. As you start and begin to run your nonprofit it will benefit, more than

Passion vs. Obsession

any other business, from your persistence. That said, it is possible to be *too* persistent— or, at least, there are the right ways to do it, and the wrong ways. Leading a charity requires you to ride the line between necessary aggressiveness and being annoying. If you're not someone for whom making asks of people and then following up with them (again and again, if necessary) comes naturally, you'll need to bite the bullet and work on that skill. If you're someone who is naturally more bullish, you may need to rein yourself in a bit so you don't push too hard and scare potential supporters off. You will need self-awareness in order to navigate this part of the process; be honest with yourself about your strengths and weaknesses, and adjust accordingly!

Something you'll need to figure out early on is your mission statement—the Why, How, and Who of your organization. Don't get too lofty with the language; your mission should be attainable and relatable.

But it should also be *inspirational*. It should tell people who you are, what you're doing, and why you're doing it, and it should also tell them why they should care and why they should support your efforts in particular. So, unless you are the first person in the universe to ever have tackled the cause you're taking on, you will need to be crystal clear about the value *you*, specifically, are bringing to it.

As you choose the language for your statement, also keep in mind that making it too fine-focused at the outset can pigeonhole you into a direction you may not want to travel. Your mission statement is going to define your non-profit now, as you launch it into the world, but it will also define you as you move forward into the future. And if you're doing things right, your organization will evolve— likely in significant ways—over time. As you get to know the population you're serving, for example, you'll likely discover that what you actually need to do in order to best address their needs is different from what you thought it would be. Or, like Good Tidings, you might end up partnering with an organization that leads you to take on a project you never would have initiated yourself but turns out to be a great fit. For this reason, your initial statement should be very broad; this will allow you the flexibility to adapt to the unexpected as your charity finds its footing.

As you move out of your first year and into your fifth and even tenth year, always be focused on executing and evolving your mission over all else—even over your top line. I know it's hard not to fall into the trap of wanting to always raise more money year over year; after all, money is what allows you to accomplish all that good work you're trying to do. But if you lose sight of your mission—if you let money itself replace your true obsession—all those donations you're raking in won't help you, because you'll be so busy chasing more that you won't be using what you have effectively. So mission first, cash second!

To set yourself apart from the dozens, hundreds, thousands of charities doing work similar to yours, you need to develop your own best practices. Don't bother trying to fit a mold; create your *own* mold. This will take time, of course, and that's okay. Be intentional about developing processes for your daily, weekly, and monthly workflow as you go. Just as every author has their own distinctive writing style and every singer has their own distinct vocal style, you should have your own leadership style. What is your unique approach for solving whatever problem happens to be at hand? What is your one and only "secret sauce"? (This is where your obsession will shine through; hard work and out-efforting everyone else never goes out of style, or unnoticed by a generous donor!)

As you try to drum up support for your nonprofit, make sure you promote your *brand*, not *yourself*. No one likes a show-off, so stay behind the scenes as much as possible and let your non-profit speak for itself. This doesn't mean that you shouldn't talk your organization up at every opportunity, though! It just means that rather than turning the focus on yourself, you need to turn it on brand recognition—the extent to which supporters can identify your logo, colors, tagline, etc.—and especially on brand awareness.

Brand awareness—in this case, the extent to which supporters are familiar with your mission, your projects, and the dates of your upcoming events—is crucial because it's what will allow your supporters to rally others to join your cause. The stronger your brand awareness, the bigger your reputation will grow, the more money you'll raise, and the more good you'll be able to do.

It's essential to know as you dive into your nonprofit venture that you are entering into one of the most competitive businesses there is. In California alone, there are 80,000 nonprofits. I say this not because I want to discourage you but because I want you to succeed—and in order to succeed, you need to know what you're getting yourself into. The fact that there are so many other nonprofits out there means you need to spend time thinking about how you are going to be unique and stand out amongst the crowd. What is your reason, your motivation, the event that's moving you to take action in this way? How can you get other people equally as excited about what you're doing as you are? Think about how you can get a potential donor, someone who has seen it all, to say "I love your approach." Be creative—and, of course, be persistent!

Chapter 3:

The Boring Stuff

As I mentioned in my preface, I won't be going into microscopic detail about the various steps you need to take in order to set up a charity in this book. But I do want to at least cover the basics here. It's not the most interesting stuff in the world, I know, but your life will end up being a whole lot easier if you heed the advice I offer in this chapter. There's no reason to fumble your way through it when you can benefit from my experience!

First of all, keep in mind that the steps required to formalize your charity differ from state to state and country to country. I live in California, so some of what I know is particular to here, but everything I'll be sharing here should be applicable across the board, no matter where you live. To figure out what else you need to know after reading this chapter, do a little research online. There are some nonprofit organizations (like CalNonprofits.org) in my state that offer wonderful online checklists and tutorials on their websites, and I'm sure there are similar resources where you live. Your state's Office of the Attorney General or Secretary of State websites should also have resources designed to guide you through the process of setting up your non-profit.

The first item you will need to lock down as you get things off the ground is your organization's name. In the United States, you must check your state's database of existing company names before registering your own name. If you're forming a nonprofit outside the US, you'll need to contact the governing body of the country where you're establishing it; every country has one (in the United Kingdom, for example, it's called the Companies House Register, and in South Africa it's the Companies and Intellectual Properties Commission).

Your name, like your mission statement, should indicate who you are but also leave room for the evolution your nonprofit will surely experience over time. You should also be prepared for the possibility that you won't get to use your first (or possibly even your second) choice. When I was forming my charity in 1995, for example, the first name I applied for was "Robin Hood Foundation"—which, I quickly found out, was already taken by a wonderful charity fighting poverty in New York City. After going back to the drawing board, I landed on "St. Nick Foundation" and tried again—only to find out that name was also was taken. Finally, I came up with "Good Tidings Foundation" . . . and we were good to go! The name has served us well over time; besides having a nice ring to it, it also has a broad enough meaning that it continues to do a great job of encompassing our ever growing and changing mission.

In the US, you don't have to file a DBA (Doing Business As) statement for a nonprofit; because you are providing a public benefit, our government grants you tax-exempt status, and your supporters will receive a tax deduction for their contributions to the extent the law allows. That said, a charity is still technically a corporation—albeit one filed under 501(c)(3) of the IRS tax code. This means that even though it is exempt from federal taxation, you still have to file IRS Form 990 every year to let the government and public know what you have done with your funds (transparency is key in the nonprofit world!). The 990 is due one month after individual returns on May 15th of each year.

In your first year, you should try to find an accounting firm who will take care of this filing, as well as registry with your state's Attorney General of Charitable Trusts, pro bono (free of charge). You'll need their services going forward, too—accounting services are not optional!—but don't expect to continue to get them for free after that first year. You should engage them for that initial pro bono work with the understanding that you will pay for their services in subsequent years. Your donors want to know that they're getting an unbiased picture of what you're spending your money on each year, and paying professional accountants to handle your finances will ensure you're doing just that.

At some point, your charity's revenue may exceed two million dollars in a single year. The good news is, you've done an amazing job raising money for your cause—congratulations! The bad news is, this means you will have to hire an independent accounting firm to perform an audit for the year—and this will cost you a minimum of $25,000. Not exactly pocket change. But like I said, this kind of audit is only necessary when you've raised a lot of money for your charity, so try not to stress about the expense; instead, think of it as a marker of your organization's success!

Many nonprofits get started without the help of an attorney. Yours can too, if you're determined to do it that way. But my recommendation is to find a law firm to guide you through the process, or at the very least assist you in an advisory role—and to find one that will do it for free.

This is the deal: Most law firms have committed themselves to take on a certain amount of pro bono hours annually for charitable causes. Your nonprofit could be the recipient of those pro bono hours; you just have to convince said firm that your organization is worthy of them. So, my advice? Put together a two-page writeup that synopsizes

what your charity is about, how its efforts will positively affect the community at large, and how this law firm will play a crucial part in making those dreams a reality. Go online and find the ten law firms closest to your charity's home base. Then go to each one and hand deliver the sealed proposal to the front desk/receptionist. For good measure, bring along a premium chocolate bar or maybe a $5 gift card to a nearby coffee shop to gift to the person you're handing the proposal to—and as you hand everything over, introduce yourself and get the name of that person. Wait three days, then follow up with a phone call. (More on this later in the book!) If you don't get an answer right away, keep calling them every three days until they give you one—always being as pleasant and gracious as possible with the person on the other end of the line, of course. If you are persistent enough and have a sense of urgency in your approach, you WILL land a lawyer/firm, and they will not charge you a penny!

If this hands-on approach makes you uncomfortable or doesn't work for you for whatever reason, another option to consider is an online service such as LegalZoom, Rocket Lawyer, IncFile, LegalNature, etc. These web-based options are very affordable, and using one of them will certainly require less time investment up front on your part. But I maintain that free is always better. I love lawyers (most of them, anyway), but why waste money that can be used for good on legal fees if you don't have to?

Some of the essential things an attorney can provide assistance with are:

1. The creation and filing of your articles of incorporation
2. Drafting your bylaws
3. Obtaining your Employer Identification Number
4. Filing for Federal and State tax exemption (including Forms 1023 and 3500)

5. Putting together other necessary disclosure statements.

This kind of work is all in their wheelhouse; they do it all the time and will already have many of the forms in template form that you can easily edit to fit the requirements/specifications of your cause, whereas if you tried to do it all yourself, you'd be starting from scratch.

You can expect at least a three- to six-month wait to get your IRS Determination Letter. There are some things you won't be able to do until you receive it, but you don't have to put everything on pause while you're waiting. For one, your initial board of directors and other "involved people" can make donations to your charity during this waiting process to get you kickstarted. You can also get started on figuring out what cloud-based storage systems you want to put in place.

You *do not* want to keep your records in an Excel spreadsheet—trust me! It may

The Boring Stuff

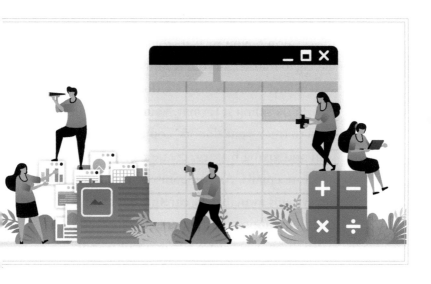

seem manageable to track things that way at first, but things are going to get complicated fast, and a spreadsheet just can't do all the things you're going to need it to do. So go for something more sophisticated from the beginning—specifically, a CRM (Customer Relationship Management) system—because if you don't, you're just going to end up having to transfer all your records over to that system later, which will be a serious headache.

In its simplest format, your system will need to track your donors' contact information and giving history, create receipts, and generate emails. As you compare the different systems available, be careful about which one you choose, as many companies offer "free" donor software for nonprofits, only to tell you once you've committed that you will need to hire them for setup and ongoing tutorials. Just on principle I don't like this, since it's a total bait-and-switch, but beyond that, from a purely practical standpoint, that kind of arrangement can end up costing you a lot of money. There are perfectly decent services out there that charge as little as fifty dollars per month; I recommend using one of those.

In your initial stages (first five years), ask yourself: *Can my nonprofit operate without paying any rent?* We were successful with that model for our first ten years—and that was before the COVID-19 pandemic, which has made a remote work environment the norm in a way that it never was before. Our first five years, we operated in our garage. Years six to ten, we obtained a free small office from the City of San Francisco at Candlestick Park after the Giants moved out to their new stadium. As a start-up, you need to do what you can to minimize costs wherever possible. So, can you work from home or provide your service in a remote fashion? If you are a direct service provider, can you take your efforts directly to your recipients? Does one of your potential partners have some extra cubicles or unused office space?

Can you get free access to one of the many coworking spaces that now exist in many hotels and office buildings? To give you an example of one way this can work, Good Tidings is a Marriott Rewards member, which allows us free usage of the WeWork coworking office space many hotels are now offering in their lobbies or restaurants.

Try to go into your launch with the goal of operating for one year without spending any cash. This is an area where the most creative will succeed. Work every angle you can think of, and see what results.

After your first year, you will want to register your charity with GuideStar and Charity Navigator, two sites that evaluate the financial health, accountability, and transparency of charities. This is important because savvy donors check these sites when they're deciding who they want to give their money to. If your charity isn't there when they do, they're going to wonder why. Following these sites' guidelines can drive donors to you and assist you in achieving maximum transparency, so do it as soon as you're eligible.

Make sure you and everyone who is joining your cause is clear on how your new company will benefit the public—whether you're targeting a small group, such as people with a very rare form of cancer, or something much more large-scale, like fighting against climate change or for social justice. The better people understand the good you're trying to do, the more motivated they'll be to help you achieve those goals.

Chapter 4:

The Board

First and foremost, this is *your* charity, which means that *you* need to keep control of your ship! Make it clear to everyone that your hope is to make this your life's work.

Your board members are the fiduciaries who will steer your organization toward a sustainable future by adopting sound, ethical, and legal governance guidelines, as well as by making sure the nonprofit has adequate resources to advance its mission.

When you're first working to build your board, you should start small—but you should also aim high, and definitely have at least one "reach" person in mind. Think of it like recruiting the best basketball team of all time: what five players will you go after? I say "five" because in my opinion, that's the perfect number for your early days. Eventually, once you see some positive revenue momentum, you'll want to ramp up the size of your board by adding some members, but five is a great number to start with.

As you assemble your board, being a good judge of character will be very beneficial. My thought early on was, *Would I entrust this person with raising my own kids?* Learning how to "scout" out this valuable intangible in people will be paramount. You need high-quality and socially current individuals who will always have your back on your team. "Duty of loyalty" issues typically arise when there is a conflict of interest between the charity's best interests and the personal interests of one of the directors—so your best bet is to make sure everyone you invite into your organization possesses the same level of unselfishness as you regarding your organization's cause.

I personally prefer not to have term limits for board members. Because of that, Good Tidings has board members that have served us for twenty-seven years, and I love that those members can draw on our history when making decisions about our present and future. The folks who have been with us since the very beginning know the hard work it took to grow to where we are, and know what it will take to get us to where we want to be tomorrow. We also have members who were once the youth we serve, which is pretty amazing.

However many board members you choose to enlist in your organization's early stages, they should be diverse—from varied backgrounds, generations, and life experiences (the board Good Tidings started out with included an eighteen-year-old, a sixty-year-old, and an accountant, among others). They should also never be compensated. If they provide a service for your charity, it should be donated, and if you do have to pay them for whatever reason, that amount should be reflected in their annual giving back to your charity.

Initially, your "Fab Five" board members shouldn't be your best pals. You will know you are doing something right when over time they *do* become your dearest friends; but you should choose each member for the value of their input, not because you go way back or like hanging out with one another. Be crystal clear with potential board members that you are interested in them for their wisdom, not their wealth; ease them into expectations, and initially use them only for advice, mentoring, and introductions. I would stay away from the "Give/Get" model, where board members have a dollar number they have to hit, as board seats should never ever be for sale. The moment you start putting demands on them, they will start putting demands on you—and that's when relationships start to deteriorate. So at the beginning, at least, keep things very light and easy.

Your very first board meeting can take place anywhere, even over a Zoom call. At this first gathering, your group will adopt the bylaws, approve the first-year budget, and basically elect each other. Make sure that during this meeting, you establish your position as not only the founder but also the chairman of the board. At that first board meeting and all meetings to follow, plan on keeping detailed minutes. You as the founder can take this on initially; if it is easier, you can even record your meetings for accuracy.

The board of directors should vigorously promote accurate fiscal management practices. Officers, directors, and employees may be liable for making, issuing, delivering, and/or publishing any report, financial statement, balance sheet, or document respecting the corporation or its assets, earnings, liabilities, contracts, or accounts that are false in any material respect, so it's vital to make sure that everything is done by the book.

From the first day, you should have Directors and Officers Insurance to protect you from the above. Nonprofit Directors & Officers (D&O) Liability insurance helps cover the defense costs, settlements, and judgments arising out of lawsuits and wrongful act allegations brought against a nonprofit organization—protecting not just the organization itself but also the personal assets of the organization's directors and board members. This is another reason that you as the founder should be on the board and insured from day one.

What makes a good board member? Well, it depends. The main thing, as I mentioned already, is to find people from diverse walks of life so you end up with a well-rounded group. I would start off by looking

at a person who is nearing retirement age and has a child who might later step in to replace her or him, since giving is usually passed down from generation to generation. You should always have at least one of these "legacy" board members in the mix. Nobody lives (or gives) forever. Good Tidings is actually planning to host a dinner for the children of our board in the coming year in order to strengthen those relationships; that's how important it is to operate with the next generation in mind.

Another good professional search category would be a CFO from a mid- to large-size company. A chief financial officer is a senior executive responsible for managing the financial actions of a company. A CFO's duties include tracking cash flow, financial planning, analyzing their company's financial strengths and weaknesses, and proposing corrective actions to address those weaknesses. Many board members won't have the interest (believe me) in spending the time needed to thoroughly look through your balance sheet and financial statement—but someone needs to do it. With this in mind, having at least one person on the board who has this skill and interest will be hugely beneficial.

Another population to consider would be someone on the younger side, say between sixteen and twenty-two years old. They will see the world in a much different light than your older members. Although they may not bring an abundance of funds to the table, they will share a valuable insight into and perspective on your mission. (They could also end up being one of those members who spends twenty-five years or more on your board.)

In addition to assembling your board, you should think about finding an official spokesperson or "voice" of your charity in your early days. This is a great way to lure an actress, athlete, or musician into getting involved with your nonprofit. All you should ask of them initially is a voice-over you can use for social media, incoming phone messages, or an end-of-the-year video, with the hopes that their involvement will grow over time. One day, if you successfully convince them that your mission is worthwhile, they may even start showing up for your programs and/or fundraising events.

Social media makes it exceptionally easy to find someone who has the same passion for your mission that you do. For us, it was NBA legend and San Francisco restauranteur Nate Thurmond, who proved to be a fantastic partner to us. Make this a priority early on: do your homework, spread your net wide, and shoot for the stars. Having name recognition on your side can only help you!

The Board

Chapter 5:

Cash Is King,

But In-Kind Is Better

One thing I learned from day one is that it is much easier to ask and receive *stuff* than it is to ask and receive money. In the twenty-seven years Good Tidings has existed, we have received well over $2,000,000 in donated goods and services.

Every charity's needs are different. Early on, make sure you evaluate the competition for funding—as in, where will you look for it and who else is after the same thing you are. You will want to develop a unique approach when it comes to taking care of your expenditures.

To begin, make a list of those expenditures you will likely have to make in your first year. (Remember, as mentioned in Chapter 3—do everything you can to avoid having to pay rent in your first year!) Hopefully between you and your board you can get at least half of your list covered through donated items. Why rely only on how far your cash will carry you when you can do so much more with donations that fill your needs?

To help with these efforts, have that young board member of yours set up all your social media avenues—Facebook, Instagram, Twitter, LinkedIn, YouTube, Vimeo, etc. You want to be as discoverable as possible online.

When it comes to getting your graphic design needs taken care of, there are many ways to tackle the situation. The simplest thing you can do is google "cheap logos";

with just a few strokes on your keyboard, you can find dozens of designers who are willing to do custom logo design for a low fee. If you want to do the extra work, you might also be able to find a creative firm who will do some pro bono work for you initially, knowing that a payday for them could come down the line—just as you did to address your legal needs when setting up your nonprofit.

Once you actually have some samples to choose from, make sure you select a brand identity that you feel can stand the test of time and looks good in all applications (in print and digital, on clothing, etc.). A good test during your logo selection process is to place your mark next to the logo of one of your partners or favorite companies. In our case, we knew we needed help with a refresh when our logo didn't stand up well next to our partners the Golden State Warriors and the San Francisco Giants.

Postage and shipping is an easy one to get donated. And although direct mail is becoming somewhat of a dinosaur, donors still like to have thank-you notes, a gift, or an annual report sent to their home; it's a personal touch that everyone seems to appreciate. My advice is to find a mid-size local company—one that would likely have a mail/shipping room—and ask them if they wouldn't mind running your charity's holiday cards through their postage machine. We have a board member who has done this for us with our annual Auction Catalogue for twenty-seven years, and I'd guess that they've saved us more than $50,000 during that time span. For a big enough company, this is a negligible expense—almost unnoticeable, really—but for your nonprofit, it will be a big help!

I know this might go against the norm, but try to always keep the mindset that you should never pay for advice when it comes to your nonprofit organization. Paying for a strategic plan or a campaign consultant is a very costly and expensive piece of overhead. In the for-profit world, this kind of investment can certainly be worthwhile, especially if it means improving your bottom line—but I have always felt that in the charity business, advice should be free. If you are ever challenged by your board or major donor to make any such expenditure, see if they feel strongly enough to underwrite it for you. If they aren't willing to do that, stand your ground and insist on at least trying to get the guidance you need without throwing money at the issue.

One great thing you'll discover as you become more and more involved in the nonprofit world is that it's full of talented people who also want to do good in the world. As you begin to connect with these folks, you'll find that many, if not all, of them will be more than willing to help you out if you ask them to, much as you would be happy to offer advice to another charity doing great work that asked *you* for advice. You started your charity with confidence; try to keep that belief alive throughout your tenure.

Remember how in Chapter 2 I mentioned that there are 112 hours in a week to get things done? That is exactly how long it should take you to create your first website—yep, just one week! There are dozens of website-building companies out there today—GoDaddy, Wix, Squarespace, WordPress, Constant Contact, Mail Chimp, Shopify, Classy, Weebly, Websight Builder, Site123, and Duda, just to name *quite* a few—and any one of these will be perfect for you at the start of your venture. These sites have templates that make website building easy enough that virtually *anyone* can do it (including you!), which means that you don't need to hire someone else to make your website for you—although getting a little pro bono help from an expert in your network of supporters so everything ends up looking as professional as possible would not be the worst idea. (This will also be a great place for that official spokesperson of yours to make a statement, providing you with immediate credibility!)

Who benefits from high administrative costs? Certainly not your mission. With that in mind, Good Tidings did not hire a full-service tax and advisory accounting firm in our early years; in fact, we didn't hire one until our *twenty-sixth* year. You may not end up waiting more than two decades yourself to do this, but you should try to stave it off when you're first getting things off the ground. Instead, when it's time to figure out what your needs are and how you can meet them without spending organization money, a great start would be to look at anything that is deemed overhead and then do an initial Fund-A-Need. Ask your supporters to donate what they can, and post about it on social media. Start with very low-cost items—cases of paper, boxes of Sharpies, file folders, etc.—and in subsequent years you can step it up a notch with items like cameras, cell phones, or whatever other items meet your charity's needs. This is both a great way to save money *and* a great way to introduce new people to your charity. Make the Fund-A-Need an annual occurrence somewhere in your fundraising calendar. Many donors like giving in this way—concrete items rather than cold, hard cash. You'll be surprised by how generous people will be, I promise. And with your donors footing the bill for these essential items, your own money will be freed up for the "doing good" part of your business.

Eventually there will come a time to pay for the items you need in order to run your charity's office and provide its programing. In Larry Harper's world, every item you could ever purchase has three price points: retail, wholesale, and charity. Take a store like Target, for example. If you walk into a Target and go over to the office supplies aisle, you'll see calculators, desk chairs, file cabinets, webcams, backpacks, and dozens of other items your charity could use. The price tag you see on these in-store items is Target's selling, or retail, price. Target, of course, paid less for those items than they're charging you—they paid wholesale. Then there's what it actually cost the manufacturer to make each item—and that, my friend, is *your* price! I am constantly going directly to the manufacturer and asking for this price. In my experience, they actually find it refreshing, because although I introduce myself as the representative of a charity, I immediately follow that introduction up with, "I am not asking for a donation, I just want to cover your cost to make the item we want."

You'd be surprised how effective this approach can be. A great example is the art studio Good Tidings recently built for our friend Alice Cooper at his new Teen Center in Mesa, AZ. Once we had our architectural plans (drafted pro bono, of course) in hand, we priced out all the items we knew we were going to need and then approached some manufacturers. In the end, we were able to build out $70,000 worth of tenant improvements for only $19,000!

Starting off your charity from the beginning with this in-kind model will make you respect and value the cash you have on hand even more. It's not about being "cheap"; it's about wanting to preserve every cent you have for your mission, the reason that your organization even exists in the first place. The better you get at finding ways to cut costs, the more time you'll be able to spend thinking about your results and outcomes rather than your income—under promise and over deliver! Mother Teresa often said, "There is no shame in asking." Always remembering to keep the best interests of the charity first ahead of anything that may benefit you personally. You run a charity—you should have no shame!

Chapter 6:

Nine to One

The word NO can be the greatest fuel for anyone's success, both in business and in life. As you build your charity, hearing "no"—and believe me, you'll hear it a lot—will be how you'll learn and eventually flourish. All prosperous people, companies, teams, organizations, etc. learn early on that "no" is really a positive, not a negative, because it makes for some of the best teaching moments you'll ever have in your life.

When I was twelve years old, I played in Sunnyslope Little League in San Gabriel, CA. Each year at Sunnyslope we held a fundraiser to benefit that year's All-Star team. You couldn't get out of participating; every player had to sell at least ten boxes of the Almond Roca candy. But there could be only one winner—the kid who sold the most boxes. And that year, the winner's prize was a Schwinn Varsity ten-speed bicycle.

Back in the '70s, if you had a Schwinn bike, you were hanging with the cool kids. And this wasn't just any Schwinn. It had *gears*—ten of them!—was orange with a black leather racing seat, and had cool drop handlebars. It was perfect.

I wanted that bike. And as I saw it, this would be quite simple; it was just a numbers game. I could win that bike by out-efforting everyone else—no special, God-given talent necessary. If I managed to go to more houses than any other kid, I would win the bike. Period.

Better yet, there was no real downside to working hard here. Even if I didn't win the bike, the worst thing that could happen was that I'd raise lots of money for my Little League—and I loved my Little League!

So off I went, house after house, neighborhood after neighborhood, knocking on doors and ringing doorbells and making my pitch over and over again. I figured out after a day or two of this that the best neighborhood to sell in was one town over, where all the well-to-do families in our area lived, and I started concentrating my efforts there. I spent as much of my free time as I possibly could canvassing that neighborhood—and needless to say, in the end, I sold almost twice as many boxes of candy as the second-place kid. That Schwinn was mine!

This is how, at twelve years old, I learned the Nine-to-One sales strategy—"Nine-to-One" as in, for every ten houses I went to, nine people said "no thank you" and just one person bought a box of candy. The trick here is, you have to be able to not take the nine noes personally, because the quicker you get through those noes, the quicker the yeses will come your way. Instead of being deflated by the no, you have to let it motivate you to keep going. (If you're wondering: I sold 456 boxes of Almond Roca, so you can do the math on how many asks I made in pursuit of that Schwinn!)

This model works for everything you will do in service of your charity. Take asking for auction items, for example: in my experience, you've got to ask for ten to get one really good item. It can be discouraging, I get it; in fact, I'm pretty sure that's why 90 percent of charities just give up on making the asks at all and go with the consignment item model instead. But don't be part of that 90 percent. Don't give up. Set yourself apart from the others by persisting. Remember, each "no" you get just means you're one step closer to getting the best auction item ever! Have the guts to trust your gut.

Obviously, nothing ever has and nothing ever will replace just asking someone personally for a donation. Even in this modern, tech-focused age (or perhaps especially because of it), people appreciate a personal touch; they want to feel seen for the contribution they're making to your cause. So make your asks as personal as possible. Take the time out to make them yourself rather than sending someone to do it in your place. Go that extra mile.

It will take time to develop your own asking style, but the more you do it, the better you will get. Getting the tone right is a bit of a balancing act: It is important to be direct and persistent, but at the same time you should never act desperate. You should be humble in your initial expectations, and when the inevitable no comes your way, be sure to accept it respectfully. Do, however, subtly express some slight disappointment when you get a no so the potential donor leaves the conversation feeling some guilt—"That's too bad, but I totally understand; thanks for your time, and if it is alright I would like to keep you up to date on what we are working on in the future." The key here is to actually follow up with that person later—in six months or a year—and show them that you've accomplished what you set out to do during the original ask. This is the way to turn a no into a yes down the road.

Many potential donors have doubts about charity start-ups. I don't know how many times people have said that I am "crazy," or have made it clear that they're not convinced I'll really be able to do what I'm saying I intend to do. Because of this, establishing trust is huge! I remember, early in my charity-building journey, asking a prominent San Francisco businessman who loved baseball for a small donation to self-publish my children's book about baseball that would be given to low-income kids. His response was, "I don't get it." My thought when I heard this was, *What do you not get about giving*

free books to kids?—but I didn't say that, obviously. Instead, I respectfully accepted his no, and three months later, once the book had seen some success, I sent him a copy. He went on to become a Good Tidings supporter. People won't always give when you most want them to, but they *will* always jump on a successful bandwagon—and hey, better late than never!

Fundraisers are, of course, a great way to raise money for your charity. Early on, try to identify a single fundraiser that you will be known for. One that hopefully can stand the test of time for decades to come. If you have no idea what this magnificent event could possibly be, then try attending other fundraisers to get ideas. You shouldn't just lift someone else's fundraiser blueprint, of course, but it's more than okay to become a *hybrid* stealer of ideas and blend the best ideas you like into one. Remember, being unique is key!

For the Good Tidings Foundation, our flagship fundraiser has always been, and still is, our Auction Catalogue. When we started back in 1995, there was no social media or online auctions. Things were a bit more . . . analog then. I had this idea of creating a beautifully laid-out book filled with amazing auction items shoppers could browse and, over a six-week period, place bids on by calling a toll-free number. I figured we could place these catalogues all over—in hotel lobbies, restaurants, gyms, coffee shops, anywhere people congregated—and in that way we could reach a wide range of folks we would otherwise be unlikely to connect with. It worked amazingly well; in fact, this single idea led us to the majority of our supporters who are still with us today.

Grants are often touted as a major source of contribution for charities but honestly, unless you have an inside track or connection, I would not waste too much time on grant writing. Many charities get caught going down this rabbit-hole, and it almost always looks grander than it is. Remember how many nonprofits I said exist in California alone? (Hint: in the tens of thousands!) Well, given that, it should come as no surprise that competition for this type of funding is compounding year over year. That said, if you do decide to pursue this route, Foundation Center, an online directory of over 150,000 grant givers in the country, would be a great place to start; it will at least provide you with some foundations in your area that may be worth sending a letter of inquiry to. And if there's any way to avoid taking this task on yourself, do! Maybe this is where a board member can jump in to help.

Let's say you put someone great on the job, they apply to a bunch of foundations, and you do get awarded some awesome grants over time. Fantastic! But make sure your charity doesn't get to a point where it relies on this type of funding in order to continue its existence. Remain as self-sufficient as possible. When economic downturns happen—and they inevitably do—grants dry up. I have seen too many charities fold during these times because those grants were their primary source of funding. So take the free money where you can get it, but make sure you have other strong financial supporters in case those grants go away at some point in the future.

Whether you're getting money through grants, wealthy donors, or more grassroots support systems, running a charity is a hustle. And every good hustler knows that they're going to hear the word "no" more often than they're going to hear the word "yes" as they work toward their goals! Just remember to use each "no" as inspiration to push forward and work harder for that next "yes," and I guarantee you will always manage to find the funds to not only keep your nonprofit afloat but actually thriving.

Chapter 7:

Howdy, Partner

Leveraging with partners and creating meaningful partnerships will drastically increase your charity's success with its mission. As I mentioned in an earlier chapter, Good Tidings partnered with the NBA's Golden State Warriors to host a holiday party for children who were living in homeless shelters in our second year of operation. Following that event, we were asked if we would be interested in partnering with them in refurbishing inner-city basketball courts.

This is where the fact that we had kept our mission statement very broad in the beginning came in quite handy. Sprucing up basketball courts wasn't something I necessarily had in mind when I launched Good Tidings, but our name clearly spelled what our intention was—to bring joy and happiness to kids, that *Spirit of the Holidays*—and, well, it seemed like playing basketball could make a lot of kids very happy! So we jumped at the opportunity, despite not knowing anything about navigating a construction project, let alone dealing with municipalities to make it happen.

Fast-forward twenty-seven years and today we have built ninety-eight courts as part of our Makin' Hoops Program with the Golden State Warriors—a program that is unprecedented in the country. And we have done the same with the Sacramento Kings and with NBA Players. We partnered with a brand that had far greater reach (and far deeper pockets!) than ours, and that gave us the opportunity not only to serve more children but also to exponentially increase awareness about our new brand.

It is almost expected that mid-size to large companies have a Social and Environmental Responsibility division, department, or at least mantra. Many corporations do an amazing job with these efforts. Take our friends at Bombas, for example: for every pair of socks, every pair of underwear, and every T-shirt they sell, they give one away—for a total of nearly 50 million items donated to date.

Bombas, clearly, has figured their philanthropy out. But many companies are lost when it comes to getting their employees engaged in a local community activity. They need a conduit to corporate responsibility—someone to help them do the good they want to do but aren't sure how to facilitate it well. This is where you come in. Reach out to some local mid-size companies that seem to be fumbling the ball when it comes to social and environmental responsibility. Offer to host a group of employees for a volunteer day, or ask the company to host something for your organization (a holiday toy drive, for example). Along the way, make sure that company's ownership group is aware of you, thus exposing people of influence directly to your mission; you never know when you'll stumble upon a future board member or major donor.

If you really want to have the best talent helping you along the way, outsourcing to the experts will be the way to go for areas like accounting, creative, and PR, among others. These kinds of highly skilled experts would be way too costly to bring on full time, but when you need something specific done, you can shop around your needs to different companies and then negotiate rates by the hour or project.

This is a great time to start thinking about offering a trade; after all, bartering is

the oldest form of doing business. Can you offer someone complimentary tickets to your upcoming gala in exchange for setting you up on QuickBooks; could a board member with a membership at a country club take a few people from a PR firm out for a day of golf in exchange for some consulting work; does someone you know have season tickets to a sporting event you could offer to someone in exchange for designing your logo? These are all great options to get things done for no cash—at least at the start.

Whomever you build partnerships with, make sure all of them are showcasing your work on their website, in their company newsletter, and amongst their employees at internal staff meetings. The better your brand awareness, the more people will want to engage with your charity—not just through work but also on their personal time. When you find new allies, be sure to share all social media handles and hashtags with them. Include images of your partners in your posts; ten people in a photo equals ten shares or likes. Where board membership in your charity is limited, the amount of partners you can accumulate is not.

Chapter 8:

It Is Better to Give

Than It is to Receive

Remember, you are in the generosity business. You started your charity because of your benevolence and kindness—because of your desire to help those who need it. This means you are likely a giver by nature. As you develop and perfect the giving effect of your cause, you also need to develop and perfect how you show your gratitude for the generosity of your donors.

Early on, I saw the value in how I thanked my supporters. Experienced givers are used to being thanked—in various ways, though the usual approach is a personal, hand-written thank-you note sent along with the receipt for their donation. But remember, we don't do "usual"; we do unique! Finding ways to thank your donors in a way they have never experienced before will set you apart and keep them giving to your cause for years to come. Good donor gifts are vital to your growth and retention.

We have gotten so good at donor gifts at Good Tidings that one board member once called us the "anti-charity," as he felt he was receiving more than he was giving. Not true of course, but—mission accomplished! Since our very first year, we have given what we call our Major Donor gift in December of each year. We have internally set that mark at cash, goods, or services donated that is valued at $5,000 or greater. We give out somewhere around sixty of these gifts each year.

It Is Better to Give Than It is to Receive

Back in 1995, when we were just starting out, we had limited resources. I had a friend in Los Angeles who did all the T-shirt screen printing for all the Warner Bros. and Disney movies. That year, the two-dozen shirts he gave me served as our Major Donor gift—a simple T-shirt, accompanied by a hand-written thank-you note, mailed in a Fund-a-Need-provided padded envelope with pro-bono postage.

In the beginning, there was no strategic motive to our thank you gifts. I was just grateful for anyone who thought what we were doing was meaningful in some way. But as we grew and found ways to give higher-quality gifts, I discovered that what we were doing was not the norm in the nonprofit world—and it was setting us apart from other charities, in a good way. Remember how I talked about our "charity price" in Chapter 5—not just wholesale but at-cost? That's the approach to take for gifts, too. Whenever you ask a company to give you a "charity price" on essential items for your charity, ask them for an auction item while you're at it. Make your pitch to enough manufacturers, and you'll find yourself in a position to give your donors very special and oftentimes custom-made gifts that you've spent as little as $25 to $40 apiece on!

Over the years, Good Tidings has given art from LeRoy Neiman, pottery from Bauer, trays from Annie Modica, blankets from Rumpl, crystal from Tiffany, mugs from Yeti, ornaments from Christopher Radko, clothing from Lululemon and on and on—thoughtful, quality gifts that our donors were actually excited to receive. We have actually become dealers and distributors for dozens of upscale brands. Now, don't get me wrong, a piece of art created by a child from a group that you serve is nice. But to be quite blunt, a crystal Tiffany bowl is way better.

In addition to giving these gifts to our generous donors, I also give out about a dozen "preemptive" donor gifts each year.

These are for people who are on the fringe, who have not contributed yet but have shown interest in what we are doing and seem close to making a generous donation. Guess what—they almost always become an annual major donor. They look forward to what the next year's gift will be, so much so that in the year that follows they make sure they are generous enough to get one. I know for a fact that this gift has encouraged folks to step up their donation game more than they otherwise would have, just because they want to make sure they get the next one. Major Donors will get F.O.M.O.

If there is only one thing you take away from reading this book—this should be it!

Chapter 8:

Saving For a Rainy Day

or Even a Pandemic

When you started your charity, you must have done so because you thought the idea was a great one. If that's the case, you should want it to continue on into the future for as long as possible, right? If so, from the very start, you must be thinking not only about how to make your cause sustainable but also constructed in a way that it can live on in perpetuity.

From the beginning, try to peel off 10 percent of your revenue or funds raised and put it aside. Initially this can be kept in a savings account or a CD. As the amount grows, you can seek out a wealth manager. Discount brokerage accounts at places like Fidelity, TD Ameritrade, Interactive Brokers, and Schwab require a very low initial investment and charge negligible fees and commissions—and wealth managers will meet with you for *free*. Set up a handful of meetings and pick their brains. You will come away with the specific knowledge that will help your cause.

The same approach goes for accounting firms. Interview four to five large, but local, accounting firms as if you are interested in hiring them. Ask for samples of their nonprofit work. Be thorough and curious, and you can learn the equivalent of a couple years' worth of college-level accounting courses in those few meetings.

Initially, I would not call this pool of money an "endowment," because this limits what you can do with it. An endowment is a gift to charity that cannot be spent in its entirety (typically, the terms permit the expenditure of income but not principal, or place a limit on the percentage or amount of the fund that can be spent in any year). So refraining from categorizing your money as an endowment will give you and your board the flexibility to use it as you see fit, though if you want to you can certainly create a one-page document establishing a policy on how it can be spent and invested.

It would be naïve to expect your charity to raise more revenue year after year in a steady climb. Unfortunately, we are all subject to the whims of the market—and trying to predict the financial future of any country is a complete guess. Just during the twenty-seven years Good Tidings has been around, the stock market has been all over the board. We started at the birth of the dot-com boom; five years later, there were double-digit losses; then there was another good run from 2003 to 2007; then a nearly 40 percent bust in 2008; then yet another good run starting in 2009; then a terrible 2018 year-end; another great year in 2019; and once again huge losses in 2020. So no, we have not consistently increased our revenue year over year; but through all of the ups and downs, a *long-term* growth of funds has always been produced.

All nonprofit leaders have lived through (and will continue to live through) the annual panic around needing to raise more money this year than you did in the last. But over a long period of time, this is, frankly, just not realistic. When I started Good Tidings we had one fundraiser: the Auction Catalogue. To try to chase that year-over-year growth, we added a farmers market, then a golf tournament, then an art and wine auction, then the Stadium Stampede, then a bocce ball tournament . . . and so on and so on.

What I quickly realized as this all unfolded was that we were ready for an endowment—a fund that could spin off the same annual income as three or four fundraisers.

You can spend a lot of money working with a fundraising consulting firm. Unless you have an underwriter for this, I would stay away from this expense. As you were when you were trying to come up with a great fundraising idea, be a hybrid stealer of ideas. Spend your time speaking with some other nonprofits who have run campaigns. Ask for them to share any creative sales pieces they used that they found successful. From there, you will need buy-in from your board—not just their vote but also some level of contribution. Next you will need to meet with the people you hope will be your two or three major donors to ask them to make a lead gift. You can tell them that your fundraising goal will be shaped by their generosity.

Think about the type of person you would want to sit down in your house and ask you for money. Would you want it to be a development person or firm? Or would you want it to be the charity's founder, a special spokesperson/celebrity connected to your cause, or possibly someone who has benefited from your charity's kindness? I think the answer is obvious.

It's fine to have a lofty fundraising goal (people love to see some flashy number). But whatever that number is, it's important to also keep in mind that whatever you raise for this endowment will be more than what you started with, and that's something to celebrate. This whole endowment thing may seem daunting, but it is not!

I held off on considering an endowment thing until, one day, a donor told me, "Your charity will die when you do." That was when I knew it was definitely time.

We had our first campaign back in 2007. We were lucky enough to have a board member who would match all gifts made, with no limit. Unfortunately, we didn't have the following then that we now have, but we still managed to raise a little over $300K;

Saving For a Rainy Day or Even a Pandemic

with the generous match from our board member, our endowment fund was born with $600,000.

Our goal all along was that unless the fund grew to some crazy number like $10,000,000, we would never touch it. It wasn't there to serve as a piggy bank; it was there to ensure that the charity would go on in some fashion after I passed. So time passed, and it just kept growing, and by 2016 it had blossomed from $600,000 to $3 million. That year, an attorney reached out to us whose (anonymous) client had instructed them to give $1 million to a charity that supported youth sports upon the occasion of her death. That attorney did a Google search and picked us—and bingo, our endowment suddenly hit $4 million.

Now we knew we were going somewhere with this thing. Bolstered by the unexpected gift we'd just received, we set out to raise an additional $5 million in 2016. The same board member who'd matched the gifts back in 2007 made a $1

million lead gift—an amazing jumping
-off point that allowed us to hit our goal.
Today, our endowment fund is $12 million.
And yes, we are turning on the cash flow;
going forward, this fund will generate over
$400,000 per year—forever!

When it comes to your own endowment, you and your board will need to
determine how much can be withdrawn each
year for use. An endowment can spin off up
to 7 percent per year, but you may decide to
withdraw less, depending on your situation.

Because we had done so much to grow
our endowment over the years, by the time
the COVID-19 pandemic hit, we were on
solid ground—so much so that we were able
to not only withstand this global crisis but
also to start a new program in support of
our friends in the Black community, specifically focused on social justice.

One great thing about having an endowment fund is that once it's established, donors
will give to it without you even having to ask,

because they'll make doing so part of their estate's planned giving. (But just because you didn't have to ask doesn't mean you don't have to offer thanks; when this time of year comes around, get ready to produce a special donor gift and organize an end-of-campaign party!)

The bottom line is, start *some* sort of cash savings for your charity, and do it from the start. Even if it is not a full-fledged endowment, it's something that you'll be able to draw on down the line. It could be what saves your neck if times get tough one day; and it could also be the financial bridge that will allow your organization to outlive you— which is what all of us want, right?

Saving For a Rainy Day or Even a Pandemic

Chapter 10:

Other Life Lessons

I've learned a lot of lessons over the past twenty-seven years, and not all of them need their own chapter. But they're still important! Here are some last thoughts and pieces of wisdom I'd like to share with you:

The best start-ups seem to grow organically; after all, you can't force greatness. As you forge your path forward, you have to be able to trust your gut, believe fate is on your side, and know you will see serendipitous success along the way.

The charity business is not an analytical business. Analytics seems to be the hot trend now, sure—but who do they really benefit? Certainly not the people you are serving. In the giving world, all they will do is slow you down. So don't think about "growth"; just think about being the *best*.

Good Tidings gets approached all the time about taking our model to the national level, but we always say no, because I am convinced that it can't be replicated on such a large scale. Our entire approach is centered on personal connections—*community* connections. If we grew too large, that would be lost. So instead of trying to expand beyond our capacity, we will continue to concentrate on the same thing we always have: getting better every year. This will keep us true to our mission and our beginnings, and will also allow us to be fluid and constantly adapting so we know we can offer help where deserving youth need it the most.

When it comes time to hire people to run your charity, I would look outside the non-profit sector—again, it's all about thinking outside the box! Of course people who have dedicated their lives to nonprofit work are fantastic folks, but anyone who's been in any single industry for too long can become entrenched in doing things a certain way. And if you've learned anything from this book, I hope it's that you need to find your own way of doing things. So, instead of trying to find someone who is bound by the "rules" of the charity world, hire someone who you have seen in action and whose work ethic and customer service skills you admire. Once you've found the right people, don't get caught up in job titles. Instead, make it clear that in your organization, everything is a team effort—that at any given time, anyone can be expected to tackle any type of task. The people who don't flinch at that are the people you want on the job.

Try to stay away from long, formal legal agreements and MOU's (Memos of Understanding). Instead, as much as possible, create "handshake" agreements from the beginning. We did two charity benefits yielding two new music studios for kids with both Jason Mraz and Kenny Loggins with just a verbal agreement over the phone. Gaining the word-of-mouth trust that will come from you consistently making good on your end of these types of agreements will make life so much easier down the road. The same goes for Strategic Plans. We have never had one, and it's never been an issue for us. If anything I think they can do more harm than good, because they give you the false belief that you can predict, and control, every expense that's going to come your way. Newsflash: at some point, there *will* be costs that you didn't expect and can't control. But instead of spinning out about it, just look at it as the cost of doing good. You can't get bummed out when you look at health insurance, accounting, or workers comp costs. They are what they are; just take them in stride and move on.

Running a charity is a constant balancing act. You always need to sweat the little things when it comes to expenditures, as we've discussed, but you also have to have your eyes on the future. Sometimes it is good to "buck the trend" when things are going well and get more conservative, and sometimes you may need to spend some money when things are tight. Again, trust your gut. Let your passion—and obsession!—guide you, and you'll get to where you want to be.

Starting this charity is who you are as a person. Everything you do for and with your charity is representative of your kind heart. As you make your way through the weeds of getting your organization up and running, never lose sight of the reason you're doing what you're doing. This is your passion, your meaning, your life's work. So enjoy every minute—which shouldn't be hard, because running a charity is the best job in the world.

Acknowledgments

Thanks to Justin Ahrens and Rule 29 for their guidance throughout this process. To Tony at O'Neil Printing for continually producing the best-quality books in the country. For all the kind people who endorsed the words in this book—thank you for your friendship and congratulations on your amazing work. To all our board members, past and present. To Tabitha Lahr for her beautiful book design. To Brooke Warner for coaching me to the finish line one more time. Finally, to Ronette, Bridgette, and Zack—thank you for your encouragement, even after I said I wouldn't write another book . . . and now, on to the next one!

About the Author

Larry Harper is the founder of the Good Tidings Foundation—a non-profit organization, now in its twenty-seventh year, that works to equally support arts, education, athletics, and wonder for marginalized children in Northern California and beyond. Since its inception, Good Tidings has built over 210 projects, awarded nearly $2M in community service scholarships, and gifted 60,000 holiday toys.

Before entering the world of philanthropy, Larry had a successful career in baseball—first as a college baseball coach, then as a scout for the San Francisco Giants. At thirty years old, after one year on the job with the Giants, he was promoted from Southern California Scout to Director of Scouting. Soon afterward, the team went to the World Series.

Over the years, Larry has received dozens of awards, including the 2018 Humanitarian of the Year Award from the Positive Coaching Alliance. He is the author of *It's The Most Wonderful Time Of The Year*, a children's book about the positive influence of baseball that has sold out three editions, as well as a memoir, *An Accidentally Amazing Life*, and a novel, *Before Jackie*. He also hosts the *Good Tidings Podcast*, a monthly production that highlights all the goodness that is happening among us. Guests of the show have included Jason Mraz, CC Sabathia, Kerri Walsh Jennings, Kenny Loggins, Ayesha Curry, Buster Posey, and many other philanthropic greats.

Larry and his wife of thirty years, Ronette, have two adult children, Zack and Bridgette, and live in Northern California.